Every Kid's Guide to
Laws that Relate to Parents and Children

Written by

JOY BERRY

CHILDRENS PRESS ®
CHICAGO

About the Author and Publisher

Joy Berry's mission in life is to help families cope with everyday problems and to help children become competent, responsible, happy individuals. To achieve her goal, she has written over two hundred self-help books for children from birth through age twelve. Her work revolutionized children's publishing by providing families with practical, how-to, living skills information that was previously unavailable in children's books.

Joy gathered a dedicated team of experts, including psychologists, educators, child developmentalists, writers, editors, designers, and artists, to form her publishing company and to help produce her work.

The company, Living Skills Press, produces thoroughly researched books and audio-visual materials that successfully combine humor and education to teach subjects ranging from how to clean a bedroom to how to resolve problems and get along with other people.

Managing Editor: Ellen Klarberg
Copy Editor: Kate Dickey
Contributing Editors: Jean Buckley, Nancy Cochran, Barbara Detrich, Frank Elia, Bob Gillen, Kathleen McBride, Susan Motycka, Gary Passarino
Editorial Assistant: Sandy Passarino

Art Director: Laurie Westdahl
Design: Abigail Johnston, Laurie Westdahl
Production: Abigail Johnston
Illustrations designed by: Bartholomew
Inker: Janie Harrison
Colorer: Janie Harrison
Composition: Curt Chelin

There are laws that apply to children.

In **EVERY KID'S GUIDE TO LAWS THAT RELATE TO PARENTS AND CHILDREN**, you will learn the following:
- some laws are specifically for children,
- some laws protect and help children,
- some laws protect and help parents,
- some laws restrict parents' control, and
- some laws emancipate children from parents.

Because you are a child, you are a *minor*. A minor is a person younger than a certain age.

The age at which you are no longer a minor varies from state to state. This age is called the *age of majority.* In some states you are a minor until you become 18. In other states you are a minor until you become 21. When you reach the age of majority, you are generally considered an adult.

Often children think that because they are minors they are not responsible for following the law. They think that only adults have to obey the law. This is not true.

According to the law, children under seven years of age are not considered intelligent enough to be responsible for the law. This is not true of children seven years of age and older. Every person over seven is expected to obey the law.

If you are like most children, you do not know about the laws you are supposed to obey. This is because very little has been written for children about the laws that relate to them. There is a lot of information about laws for teenagers and young adults, but not much has been written for children.

This book is for children. It doesn't deal with *all* the laws that apply to minors. Instead, it deals with laws that relate to parents and children between seven and thirteen.

Many of the laws that concern you and your relationship with your parents or guardians have been established to protect you. According to the law, your parents or guardians must *support* you. They must see that you have food, clothing, and shelter.

Your parents or guardians must also **protect** you. They must do everything they can to see that you are kept healthy and safe.

According to the law, your parents or guardians must *educate* you. They must make sure that you go to school or are educated in a way that is acceptable to society.

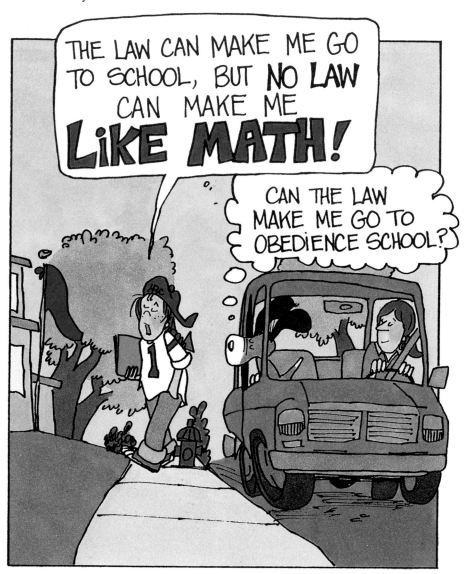

Your parents or guardians must also *control* you.
They must do everything they can to see that you do
not harm yourself, other people, or other people's
property.

It is against the law for your parents or guardians to *neglect* you. If your parents or guardians fail to support, protect, educate, or control you, they are neglecting you and therefore are disobeying the law.

It is also against the law for your parents or guardians to **abuse** you. They cannot do *anything* that will injure you. This includes emotional, physical, and sexual abuse.

Sometimes it is hard to know if a parent or guardian neglected or abused a child.

It is especially hard for children to determine this by themselves.

If you think you are being neglected or abused, talk to your parents or guardians about it when they are calm or in a good mood. If they do not agree with you or do not change their behavior, talk to another caring adult about it.

You can talk to someone like a
- teacher,
- principal,
- minister,
- close relative (a grandparent, aunt, or uncle), or
- close adult friend.

Be sure to choose someone you can trust, and do not lie or exaggerate. Telling the truth in these situations is very important if you want help for yourself and your parents or guardians.

If your parents or guardians have not neglected or abused you, the person you talk to can assure you of that fact and help you understand your parents' or guardians' behavior.

If your parents or guardians *have* neglected or abused you, the person you talk to will get help for you and your parents or guardians.

It would be difficult, if not impossible, for your parents or guardians to support, protect, educate, and control you if you ran away from home.

Therefore, it is against the law for you to leave home permanently without your parents' or guardians' permission.

Some of the laws that relate to you at home have been established to help your parents or guardians do their job. According to the law, your parents or guardians have the right to *control* you.

This means that, according to the law, your parents or guardians can decide whom you can and cannot be with. In other words, your parents or guardians can legally choose the kinds of friends you have.

According to the law, your parents or guardians can also control what you can and cannot do, as long as it does not endanger your safety or morals. (Morals are your feelings of right and wrong).

This includes chores around the house. Your parents or guardians have the right to have you help out and work at home.

According to the law, your parents or guardians can control when you can do things.

Your parents or guardians can also control where you can and cannot go.

According to the law, your parents or guardians can control where you work, as long as they do not violate the child labor laws.

The law entitles your parents or guardians to keep the money you earn. This means that the money you earn belongs to your parents unless they allow you to keep it. There are a few exceptions to this law. For example, if you work in films or on television, your parents or guardians must save your earnings for you. They must give it to you when you are old enough to use it responsibly.

To help your parents or guardians control you, the law gives them the right to **discipline** you. This means that your parents or guardians can, whenever necessary, isolate you (keep you away from someone or something).

Whenever necessary, your parents or guardians can deprive you (not let you have something you want or do something you want to do) as long as they are not being abusive.

Your parents or guardians can, whenever necessary, require that you do something you do not want to do, as long as it does not endanger your safety or morals.

Whenever necessary, your parents or guardians can physically punish you. Spanking is an example of physical punishment. Your parents or guardians can discipline you as they see fit, as long as the punishment does not go beyond what a reasonable parent or guardian would do under the same circumstances. Parents or guardians who discipline their children excessively are abusing their children and are breaking the law.

In what ways do your parents or guardians control you?

- Who chooses your friends?
- Who decides what programs you watch on TV?
- Who decides what kind of clothes you wear?
- Who decides what jobs you do around the house?
- Who decides where you work?
- Who decides whether you keep the money you earn?
- Who decides when you go to bed at night?
- Who decides where you go after school and on weekends?

As you answered the questions on the preceding page, you might have discovered that *you* have a lot of control over the things you do. If this is true, you need to know that you have control because your parents or guardians have given it to you.

The law allows a parent or guardian to be in control of a child's life. Some parents or guardians choose to be in complete control of their children. Other parents or guardians give some control to their children if they are able to handle it responsibly.

If your parents or guardians have given you control over certain things in your life, you need to handle them responsibly and wisely. If you do not, your parents or guardians have the right and the responsibility to take back control of your life.

You might resist your parents' or guardians' control and, as a consequence, do something that hurts yourself and others.

If and when this happens, you can be held responsible for your wrongdoings.

According to the law, minors over the age of seven are legally responsible for wrongs done by them *except* in these situations:

1. A child does something wrong under the suggestion, encouragement, or direction of his or her parent or guardian.

2. A parent or guardian gives his or her child
   permission to do something that is wrong.

3. A parent's or guardian's negligence allows a child to do something wrong.

4. A parent or guardian knows about a child's harmful or destructive tendency and fails to do anything to stop or control it.

The laws that relate to you at home apply until you reach the age of majority (become 18 or 21, depending upon the state) or you are *emancipated*.

You can be emancipated by your parents or
guardians if

- your parents or guardians give up their right to
  you (this includes the rights to services and
  earnings) or
- you agree to give up the support and protection of
  your parents.

In order for you to be emancipated, you must be
- old enough to work (usually age 16) and
- be able to care for yourself and your own needs.

A minor cannot legally emancipate himself or herself without the consent of the parent or guardian.

A parent or guardian cannot emancipate a minor without the minor being ready and willing to be emancipated. Both parents or guardians and the minor must agree on emancipation before a child can be emancipated.

Parents or guardians can, at any point, voluntarily agree to allow other responsible adults to care for their children, such as a relative, friend, or foster parent. But this does not end their responsibility to support and educate their child.

Under special circumstances the court of law can end a parent's or guardian's authority over a child. If necessary, minors may be separated from their parents or guardians by the court and put in the care of other adults or an institution.

The laws that you have learned about in this book have been established so that you and the people around you can lead safe, productive lives. For this reason . . .